FIRST 50 SONGS

YOU SHOULD PLAY ON THE VIBRAPHONE

Arrangements by Will Rapp

ISBN 978-1-5400-6102-7

For all works contained herein:
Unauthorized copying, arranging, adapting, recording, Internet posting, public performance,
or other distribution of the music in this publication is an infringement of copyright.
Infringers are liable under the law.

Visit Hal Leonard Online at
www.halleonard.com

Contact us:
Hal Leonard
7777 West Bluemound Road
Milwaukee, WI 53213
Email: info@halleonard.com

In Europe, contact:
Hal Leonard Europe Limited
42 Wigmore Street
Marylebone, London, W1U 2RN
Email: info@halleonardeurope.com

In Australia, contact:
Hal Leonard Australia Pty. Ltd.
4 Lentara Court
Cheltenham, Victoria, 3192 Australia
Email: info@halleonard.com.au

ALL OF ME

Vibraphone

Words and Music by SEYMOUR SIMONS
and GERALD MARKS

Copyright © 1931 Sony/ATV Music Publishing LLC, Round Hill Songs, Marlong Music Corp. and Bourne Co. (ASCAP)
Copyright Renewed
All Rights on behalf of Sony/ATV Music Publishing LLC Administered by Sony/ATV Music Publishing LLC, 424 Church Street, Suite 1200, Nashville, TN 37219
International Copyright Secured   All Rights Reserved

ALL THE THINGS YOU ARE
from VERY WARM FOR MAY

Vibraphone

Lyrics by OSCAR HAMMERSTEIN II
Music by JEROME KERN

Copyright © 1939 UNIVERSAL - POLYGRAM INTERNATIONAL PUBLISHING, INC.
Copyright Renewed
All Rights Reserved   Used by Permission

AUTUMN IN NEW YORK

VIBRAPHONE

Words and Music by
VERNON DUKE

Ballad

Copyright © 1934 KAY DUKE MUSIC
Copyright Renewed
All Rights Controlled and Administered by UNIVERSAL MUSIC CORP.
All Rights Reserved   Used by Permissio

AUTUMN LEAVES

Vibraphone

English lyric by JOHNNY MERCER
French lyric by JACQUES PREVERT
Music by JOSEPH KOSMA

© 1947, 1950 (Renewed) ENOCH ET CIE
Sole Selling Agent for U.S. and Canada: MORLEY MUSIC CO., by agreement with ENOCH ET CIE
All Rights Reserved

BAGS' GROOVE

VIBRAPHONE

By MILT JACKSON

Copyright © 1958 (Renewed 1986) Reecie Music
International Copyright Secured   All Rights Reserved

BASIN STREET BLUES

VIBRAPHONE

Words and Music by
by SPENCER WILLIAMS

© 1928, 1929, 1933 (Renewed) EDWIN H. MORRIS & COMPANY, A Division of MPL Music Publishing, Inc.
All Rights Reserved

BIRDLAND

VIBRAPHONE

By JOSEF ZAWINUL

Fast rock

Copyright © 1976 MULATTO MUSIC
Copyright Renewed
All Rights Controlled and Administered by SONGS OF UNIVERSAL, INC.
All Rights Reserved   Used by Permission

BODY AND SOUL

VIBRAPHONE

Words by EDWARD HEYMAN,
ROBERT SOUR and FRANK EYTON
Music by JOHN GREEN

Ballad

Copyright © 1930 Warner Bros. Inc.
Copyright renewed; extended term of Copyright deriving from Edward Heyman assigned and effective January 1, 1987 to Range Road Music Inc. and Quartet Music
Extended term of Copyright deriving from John Green, Robert Sour and Frank Eyton assigned to Warner Bros. Inc. and Druropetal Music
All Rights for Quartet Music Administered by BMG Rights Management (US) LLC
International Copyright Secured   All Rights Reserved
Used by Permission

CHEROKEE
(Indian Love Song)

VIBRAPHONE

Words and Music by
RAY NOBLE

Copyright © 1938 The Peter Maurice Music Co., Ltd., London, England
Copyright Renewed and Assigned to Shapiro, Bernstein & Co., Inc., New York for U.S.A. and Canada
International Copyright Secured All Rights Reserved
Used by Permission

CAN'T STOP THE FEELING!
from TROLLS

Vibraphone

Words and Music by JUSTIN TIMBERLAKE,
MAX MARTIN and SHELLBACK

Copyright © 2016 by Universal Music - Z Tunes LLC, Tennman Tunes, DWA Songs and MXM
All Rights for Tennman Tunes Administered by Universal Music - Z Tunes LLC
All Rights for DWA Songs Administered by Almo Music Corp.
All Rights for MXM Administered Worldwide by Kobalt Songs Music Publishing
International Copyright Secured   All Rights Reserved

CLAIR DE LUNE

VIBRAPHONE

By CLAUDE DEBUSSY

Slowly, with rubato

Copyright © 2019 by HAL LEONARD LLC
International Copyright Secured All Rights Reserved

DON'T GET AROUND MUCH ANYMORE

Vibraphone

Words and Music by
DUKE ELLINGTON
and BOB RUSSELL

Copyright © 1942, 1943 Sony/ATV Music Publishing LLC and Harrison Music Corp.
Copyright Renewed
All Rights on behalf of Sony/ATV Music Publishing LLC Administered by Sony/ATV Music Publishing LLC, 424 Church Street, Suite 1200, Nashville, TN 37219
All Rights on behalf of Harrison Music Corp. Administered by Music Sales Corporation
International Copyright Secured   All Rights Reserved

DESAFINADO

Vibraphone

Original Text by NEWTON MENDONÇA
Music by ANTONIO CARLOS JOBIM

Copyright © 1959, 1962 Editora Musical Arapua
All Rights for the U.S. Administered by Corcovado Music Corp. and Bendig Music Corp.
All Rights for Canada Administered by Bendig Music Corp.
International Copyright Secured   All Rights Reserved

FLY ME TO THE MOON
(In Other Words)

Vibraphone

Words and Music by
BART HOWARD

Moderate Swing

TRO - © Copyright 1954 (Renewed) Palm Valley Music, L.L.C., New York, NY
International Copyright Secured
All Rights Reserved Including Public Performance For Profit
Used by Permission

THE FOOL ON THE HILL

Vibraphone

Words and Music by JOHN LENNON
and PAUL McCARTNEY

Slowly

Half Pedal

Copyright © 1967 Sony/ATV Music Publishing LLC
Copyright Renewed
All Rights Administered by Sony/ATV Music Publishing LLC, 424 Church Street, Suite 1200, Nashville, TN 37219
International Copyright Secured All Rights Reserved

FRIEND LIKE ME

from ALADDIN

VIBRAPHONE

Music by ALAN MENKEN
Lyrics by HOWARD ASHMAN

© 1992 Wonderland Music Company, Inc. and Walt Disney Music Company
All Rights Reserved. Used by Permission.

Half Pedal

Half Pedal

HAVE YOU MET MISS JONES?

Vibraphone

Words by LORENZ HART
Music by RICHARD RODGERS

Copyright © 1937 (Renewed) by Chappell & Co.
Rights for the Extended Renewal Term in the U.S. Controlled by Williamson Music c/o Concord Music Publishing and WC Music Corp.
International Copyright Secured   All Rights Reserved

THE GIRL FROM IPANEMA
(Garôta De Ipanema)

VIBRAPHONE

Music by ANTONIO CARLOS JOBIM
English Words by NORMAN GIMBELL
Original Words by VINICIUS DE MORAES

Copyright © 1963 ANTONIO CARLOS JOBIM and VINICIUS DE MORAES, Brazil
Copyright Renewed 1991 and Assigned to SONGS OF UNIVERSAL, INC. and WORDS WEST LLC
English Words Renewed 1991 by NORMAN GIMBEL for the World and Assigned to WORDS WEST LLC (P.O. Box 15187, Beverly Hills, CA 90209 USA)
All Rights Reserved   Used by Permission

HAPPY

from DESPICABLE ME 2

VIBRAPHONE

Words and Music by
PHARRELL WILLIAMS

Moderately fast

Copyright © 2013 EMI April Music Inc., More Water From Nazareth and Universal Pictures Global Music
All Rights on behalf of EMI April Music Inc. and More Water From Nazareth Administered by Sony/ATV Music Publishing LLC, 424 Church Street, Suite 1200, Nashville, TN 37219
All Rights on behalf of Universal Pictures Global Music Controlled and Administered by Universal Music Works
International Copyright Secured   All Rights Reserved

HARLEM NOCTURNE

Vibraphone

Words by EARL HAGEN
Music by DICK ROGERS

Copyright © 1940, 1946, 1951 Shapiro, Bernstein & Co., Inc., New York
Copyright Renewed
International Copyright Secured All Rights Reserved
Used by Permission

HAVANA

Vibraphone

Words and Music by CAMILA CABELLO,
LOUIS BELL, PHARRELL WILLIAMS, ADAM FEENEY,
ALI TAMPOSI, JEFFREY LAMAR WILLIAMS, BRIAN LEE,
ANDREW WOTMAN, BRITTANY HAZARD and KAAN GUNESBERK

Latin groove

Copyright © 2017 Maidmetal Limited, Milamoon Songs, Sony/ATV Music Publishing (UK), EMI April Music Inc., EMI Pop Music Publishing, More Water From Nazareth, EMI Blackwood Music Inc.,
EMI Music Publishing Ltd., Nyankingmusic, Sam Fam Beats, Reservoir 416, Young Stoner Life Publishing LLC, Andrew Watt Music, People Over Planes, These Are Songs Of Pulse,
Warner-Tamerlane Publishing Corp., Songs From The Dong, 300 Rainwater Music, Atlantic Songs, Warner-Tamerlane Publishing Corp. and Kaan Gunesberk Publishing Designee
All Rights on behalf of Maidmetal Limited, Milamoon Songs, Sony/ATV Music Publishing (UK), EMI April Music Inc., EMI Pop Music Publishing, More Water From Nazareth, EMI Blackwood Music Inc.,
EMI Music Publishing Ltd., Nyankingmusic and Sam Fam Beats Administered by Sony/ATV Music Publishing LLC, 424 Church Street, Suite 1200, Nashville, TN 37219
All Rights on behalf of Reservoir 416 and Young Stoner Life Publishing LLC Administered Worldwide by Reservoir Media Management, Inc.
All Rights on behalf of Songs From The Dong, 300 Rainwater Music and Atlantic Songs Administered by Warner-Tamerlane Publishing Corp.
All Rights on behalf of Andrew Watt Music Administered Worldwide by Songs Of Kobalt Music Publishing
All Rights on behalf of People Over Planes Administered by These Are Songs Of Pulse
International Copyright Secured   All Rights Reserved

HEY THERE

VIBRAPHONE

Words and Music by RICHARD ADLER
and JERRY ROSS

© Copyright 1954 (Renewed 1982) J & J Ross Company LLC and Lakshmi Puja Music Ltd.
All Rights Reserved   Used by Permission

IN A MELLOW TONE

Vibraphone

By DUKE ELLINGTON

Copyright © 1940, 1942 Sony/ATV Music Publishing LLC in the U.S.A.
Copyright Renewed
All Rights on behalf of Sony/ATV Music Publishing LLC Administered by Sony/ATV Music Publishing LLC, 424 Church Street, Suite 1200, Nashville, TN 37219
Rights for the world outside the U.S.A. Administered by EMI Robbins Catalog Inc. (Publishing) and Alfred Music (Print)
International Copyright Secured All Rights Reserved

HOW FAR I'LL GO
from MOANA

VIBRAPHONE

Music and Lyrics by
LIN-MANUEL MIRANDA

© 2016 Walt Disney Music Company
All Rights Reserved. Used by Permission.

ISN'T IT ROMANTIC?

from the Paramount Picture LOVE ME TONIGHT

Vibraphone

Words by LORENZ HART
Music by RICHARD RODGERS

Easy swing

Copyright © 1932 Sony/ATV Music Publishing LLC
Copyright Renewed
All Rights Administered by Sony/ATV Music Publishing LLC, 424 Church Street, Suite 1200, Nashville, TN 37219
International Copyright Secured   All Rights Reserved

It Don't Mean a Thing
(If It Ain't Got That Swing)

Vibraphone

Words and Music by DUKE ELLINGTON
and IRVING MILLS

Copyright © 1932 Sony/ATV Music Publishing LLC and EMI Mills Music, Inc. in the U.S.A.
Copyright Renewed
All Rights on behalf of Sony/ATV Music Publishing LLC Administered by Sony/ATV Music Publishing LLC, 424 Church Street, Suite 1200, Nashville, TN 37219
Rights for the world outside the U.S.A. Administered by EMI Mills Music, Inc. (Publishing) and Alfred Music (Print)
International Copyright Secured   All Rights Reserved

JA-DA

VIBRAPHONE

Words and Music by
BOB CARLETON

Copyright © 2019 by HAL LEONARD LLC
International Copyright Secured All Rights Reserved

THE LOOK OF LOVE

from *CASINO ROYALE*

VIBRAPHONE

Words and Music by HAL DAVID
and BURT BACHARACH

Copyright © 1967 Colgems-EMI Music Inc.
Copyright Renewed
All Rights Administered by Sony/ATV Music Publishing LLC, 424 Church Street, Suite 1200, Nashville, TN 37219
International Copyright Secured   All Rights Reserved

MISTY

VIBRAPHONE

Music by
ERROLL GARNER

Ballad

Copyright © 1954 by Octave Music Publishing Corp.
Copyright Renewed
All Rights Administered by Downtown DLJ Songs
All Rights Reserved   Used by Permission

MOOD INDIGO

Vibraphone

Words and Music by DUKE ELLINGTON,
IRVING MILLS and ALBANY BIGARD

Copyright © 1931 Sony/ATV Music Publishing LLC, EMI Mills Music, Inc. and Indigo Mood Music in the U.S.A.
Copyright Renewed
All Rights on behalf of Sony/ATV Music Publishing LLC Administered by Sony/ATV Music Publishing LLC, 424 Church Street, Suite 1200, Nashville, TN 37219
Rights for the world outside the U.S.A. Administered by EMI Mills Music, Inc. (Publishing) and Alfred Music (Print)
International Copyright Secured All Rights Reserved

MOONLIGHT IN VERMONT

Vibraphone

Words by JOHN BLACKBURN
Music by KARL SUESSDORF

Copyright © 1944 (Renewed 1972) Michael H. Goldsen, Inc.
Copyright Renewed 2000 Michael H. Goldsen, Inc. and Johnny R. Music Company (c/o The Songwriters Guild Of America)
All Rights in the Western Hemisphere outside the U.S. Controlled by Michael H. Goldsen, Inc.
International Copyright Secured   All Rights Reserved

MORNING DANCE

VIBRAPHONE

By JAY BECKENSTEIN

© 1979 Harlem Music, Inc. and Crosseyed Bear Music (BMI)
Administered by Shelly Bay Music, 423 Mountainview Road, Englewood, NJ 07631
International Copyright Secured All Rights Reserved

MY ROMANCE

Vibraphone

Words by LOREZ HART
Music by RICHARD RODGERS

Copyright © 1935 by Williamson Music Company and Lorenz Hart Publishing Co.
Copyright Renewed
All Rights in the U.S. Administered by Williamson Music Company c/o Concord Music Publishing
International Copyright Secured All Rights Reserved

ON GREEN DOLPHIN STREET

Vibraphone

Lyrics by NED WASHINGTON
Music by BRONISLAU KAPER

Copyright © 1947 Primary Wave Songs, Catharine Hinen Music and Patti Washington Music
Copyright Renewed
All Rights for Primary Wave Songs Administered by BMG Rights Management (US) LLC
All Rights for Catharine Hinen Music Controlled by Shapiro, Bernstein & Co., Inc.
Exclusive Print Rights for Patti Washington Music Administered by Alfred Music
All Rights Reserved   Used by Permission

NIGHT TRAIN

VIBRAPHONE

Words by OSCAR WASHINGTON and LEWIS C. SIMPKINS
Music by JIMMY FORREST

Copyright © 1952 (Renewed) by Embassy Music Corporation (BMI)
International Copyright Secured All Rights Reserved
Reprinted by Permission

THE PINK PANTHER

from THE PINK PANTHER

Vibraphone

By HENRY MANCINI

Copyright © 1963 Northridge Music Company and EMI U Catalog Inc.
Copyright Renewed
All Rights on behalf of Northridge Music Company Administered by Spirit Two Music
Exclusive Print Rights for EMI U Catalog Inc. Controlled and Administered by Alfred Music
All Rights Reserved   Used by Permission

PURE IMAGINATION

from WILLY WONKA AND THE CHOCOLATE FACTORY

Vibraphone

Words and Music by LESLIE BRICUSSE
and ANTHONY NEWLEY

Copyright © 1970 Taradam Music, Inc.
Copyright Renewed
All Rights Administered by Downtown Music Publishing LLC
All Rights Reserved   Used by Permission

ST. THOMAS

VIBRAPHONE

By SONNY ROLLINS

Copyright © 1963 Prestige Music c/o Concord Music Publishing
Copyright Renewed
All Rights Reserved   Used by Permission

SATIN DOLL

VIBRAPHONE

By DUKE ELLINGTON

Copyright © 1953 Sony/ATV Music Publishing LLC
Copyright Renewed
All Rights Administered by Sony/ATV Music Publishing LLC, 424 Church Street, Suite 1200, Nashville, TN 37219
International Copyright Secured   All Rights Reserved

SHAKE A TAIL FEATHER

Vibraphone

Written by OTHA HAYES,
VERLIE RICE and ANDRE WILLIAMS

Rockin'

Half Pedal

Copyright © 1963 Vapac Music Publishing, Inc.
Copyright Renewed
All Rights Controlled and Administered by Spirit One Music
International Copyright Secured   All Rights Reserved

Sing

VIBRAPHONE

Words and Music by
JOE RAPOSO

Driving, show style

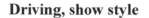

Copyright © 1971 by Jonico Music, Inc.
Copyright Renewed
All Rights in the U.S.A. Administered by Green Fox Music, Inc.
International Copyright Secured   All Rights Reserved

SOMEWHERE, MY LOVE

Lara's Theme from DOCTOR ZHIVAGO

VIBRAPHONE

Lyric by PAUL FRANCIS WEBSTER
Music by MAURICE JARRE

© 1965, 1966 (Renewed 1993, 1994) Webster Music Co. and EMI Robbins Catalog Inc.
All Rights for Webster Music Co. outside the U.S. and Canada Administered by Almo Music Corp.
All Rights for EMI Robbins Catalog Inc. Administered by EMI Robbins Catalog Inc. (Publishing) and Alfred Music (Print)
International Copyright Secured   All Rights Reserved

SOPHISTICATED LADY

Vibraphone

Words and Music by DUKE ELLINGTON,
IRVING MILLS and MITCHELL PARISH

Copyright © 1933 Sony/ATV Music Publishing LLC and EMI Mills Music Inc. in the U.S.A.
Copyright Renewed
All Rights on behalf of Sony/ATV Music Publishing LLC Administered by Sony/ATV Music Publishing LLC, 424 Church Street, Suite 1200, Nashville, TN 37219
All Rights on behalf of EMI Mills Music Inc. Administered by EMI Mills Music Inc. (Publishing) and Alfred Music (Print)
International Copyright Secured   All Rights Reserved

WHAT ARE YOU DOING THE REST OF YOUR LIFE

VIBRAPHONE

Lyrics by ALAN and MARILYN BERGMAN
Music by MICHEL LEGRAND

© 1969 (Renewed) UNITED ARTISTS MUSIC COMPANY INC.
All Rights Controlled by EMI U CATALOG INC. (Publishing) and ALFRED MUSIC (Print)
All Rights Reserved   Used by Permission

SWAY
(Quien Sera)

VIBRAPHONE

English Words by NORMAN GIMBEL
Spanish Words and Music by PABLO BELTRAN RUIZ
and LUIS DEMETRIO TRANCONIS MOLINAS

Copyright © 1954 by Editorial Mexicana De Musica Internacional, S.A. and Words West LLC (P.O. Box 15187, Beverly Hills, CA 90209, USA)
Copyright Renewed
All Rights for Editorial Mexicana De Musica Internacional, S.A. Administered by Peer International Corporation
International Copyright Secured   All Rights Reserved

SWEET CAROLINE

Vibraphone

Words and Music by
NEIL DIAMOND

Copyright © 1969 Stonebridge-Music, Inc.
Copyright Renewed
All Rights Administered by UNIVERSAL TUNES
All Rights Reserved   Used by Permission

THE SWINGIN' SHEPHERD BLUES

VIBRAPHONE

Words and Music by MOE KOFFMAN,
RHODA ROBERTS and KENNY JACOBSON

Laid-back blues

Copyright © 1958 EMI Longitude Music
Copyright Renewed
All Rights Administered by Sony/ATV Music Publishing LLC, 424 Church Street, Suite 1200, Nashville, TN 37219
International Copyright Secured   All Rights Reserved

TREASURE

Vibraphone

Words and Music by BRUNO MARS, ARI LEVINE,
PHILIP LAWRENCE, FREDRICK BROWN,
THIBAUT BERLAND and CHRISTOPHER ACITO

© 2012 BMG GOLD SONGS, MARS FORCE MUSIC, UNIVERSAL MUSIC CORP., TOY PLANE MUSIC, NORTHSIDE INDEPENDENT MUSIC PUBLISHING LLC, WC MUSIC CORP.,
ROC NATION MUSIC, MUSIC FAMAMANEM, CONCORD SOUNDS o/b/o BECAUSE EDITIONS, HEADBANGERS PUBLISHING and LICKSHOT c/o CONCORD MUSIC PUBLISHING
All Rights for BMG GOLD SONGS and MARS FORCE MUSIC Administered by BMG RIGHTS MANAGEMENT (US) LLC
All Rights for TOY PLANE MUSIC Controlled and Administered by UNIVERSAL MUSIC CORP.
All Rights for ROC NATION MUSIC and MUSIC FAMAMANEM Administered by WC MUSIC CORP.
All Rights Reserved   Used by Permission

WALKIN' ON THE SUN

Vibraphone

Words and Music by GREG CAMP, PAUL DE LISLE.
STEVE HARWELL and KEVIN IANNELLO

Copyright © 2004 Sno Cone Music Publishing Words Squish Moth Music
All Rights Controlled and Administered by Spirit One Music
All Rights Reserved   Used by Permission

Half Pedal

WHEN SUNNY GETS BLUE

VIBRAPHONE

Lyric by JACK SEGAL
Music by MARVIN FISHER

Copyright © 1956 Sony/ATV Music Publishing LLC
Copyright Renewed
All Rights Administered by Sony/ATV Music Publishing LLC, 424 Church Street, Suite 1200, Nashville, TN 37219
International Copyright Secured   All Rights Reserved